MERCANTILISM IN THE EUROPE OF THE 1990S

A BRIEF ESSAY

Elena Scarfagna Rossi

2018©Elena Scarfagna Rossi

ISBN: 9781719865357

First publication January 1996, Hull University

esrwriter@gmail.com

Independent publication

All rights reserved

It is usual to describe the earliest stages of capitalism as mercantilism, the word denoting the central importance of the merchant overseas traders who rose to prominence in 17th and 18th century England, Germany, and the Low Countries.

In numerous pamphlets these merchants defended the principle that their trading activities buttressed the interest of the sovereign power, even when, to the consternation of the court, this required sending "treasures" (bullion) abroad. Treasure used in this way became itself a commodity in foreign trade, in which, as the great merchant Thomas Mun wrote about 1630, "we must ever observe this rule; to sell more to strangers than we consume of theirs in value." For all its trading mentality, mercantilism was only partially a market-co-ordinated system. Government monopolies granted exclusive trading rights to groups such as the East India or the Turkey companies. Mercantilist economies relied on regulated, not free, prices and wages.

In *The Wealth of Nations* the libertarian and philosopher Adam Smith described the dynamics and the coordinative processes of capitalism, entrusted to the market mechanism which is curbed and contained by the condition of competition. Smith perceived the market as a means of solving the economic problem. Competitive search for capital accumulation would impart a distinctive tendency to a society that harnessed its motive force. The expansion of firms created the possibility of an even finer division of labour which improved profits by lowering the costs of production, thereby encouraging the further enlargement of the firms. In this way the incentive of the market system gave rise to the augmentation of the wealth of the nation itself.

Under capitalism two realms of authority existed where there had formerly been only one, a realm of political governance for such purposes as war or law and order and a realm of economic governance over the processes of production and distribution.

The influence of mercantilist beliefs through to the last decades can still be found in Europe, especially explicated in the economic rivalry between the super-powers.

Contemporary mercantilism consists in particular state regulations and interventions directed at gaining national advantage over other both economic and political powers. Through improved market system Europe developed an affluent way of life which makes the continent dependent upon the outside world, both for many of the raw materials upon which its economy is based, and for export markets from which to earn the funds to pay for them. During the last decades Europe has realised a new commercial and economic relationship with the Commonwealth countries by introducing a single generalised system of trade preferences in favour of the developing world as a whole. Anglophone and Francophone Africa enjoy a new trade and aid link thanks to the Lomé Convention, which encourages and facilitates exportations in Europe. In fact, the European Community bridges the gap between

North and South, supplying 40% of all economic aid to developing countries, and absorbing a quarter of all their exports. Today Europe emerging power is essentially economic, commercial, and cultural. If we consider the increasing preponderance of economic questions in the political attitudes, we see how these questions are decided by the productive power of our economies, by their capacity to sustain a rapid and steady growth of international trade and investment.

Mercantilism includes wealth accumulation and the pursuit of a national advantage in the control of economic resources and markets in the international system. The state power is seen as dependent on such control, and the international economy as involving rivalry between states. Contemporary mercantilism, as the 17th century one, requires a strong domestic market, a large population to supply labour, and an army to secure markets and colonial territories. Colonies are seen as passive victims in such an economic process. Colonial territories are important as possible markets for manufactured goods and as sources of raw materials. In its earlier stages mercantilist economic politics prohibited manufacturing in the colonies for this purpose. In this perspective mercantilism can be seen as the subordination of business and private enterprises as tools for the pursuit of state power. Such a condition can be gained through a gradual transformation of national economic resources by using legislaticns and taking political steps.

The "great illusion" of indefinite economic well-being and stability, fostered during the later 1950s and 1960s, was shattered by a succession of shocks that assailed the global economy from the early 1970s onwards. By the mid 1980s the global economy had experienced growing currency crises, accelerating inflation, shock oil price increases, the growing indebtedness of many Less Developed Countries, induced recession, unemployment and fear of a protectionist epidemic. Currency crises reflected inflationary pressures and intensified international economic competition. These changes manifested themselves in the international monetary system. During 1973-74 the Organisation of Petroleum

Exporting Countries increased enormously the price of crude oil. The effects of the oil crisis of 1973-74 caused concerns about the reliability of supplies of this energy source, increased oil bill for oil importing nations, and finally huge sums of foreign currency possessed by the oil exporting countries but placed on deposit in the international banking system. At this point mercantilist measures in Europe were promoted to increase the power of the states and their rulers against other communities with which conflicts of interest, and arms, might have developed.

Classical mercantilism was seen as a policy directed towards the accumulation of bullion, spices and all other readily transportable forms of wealth that might be used for recruiting and sustain armed forces. Contemporary European mercantilism protects the society`s economic strength and the strategically advantageous balance of trade with other countries. The extensive, and often intensive, governmental involvement in many areas of economic and society is a response to the chronic uncertainties of both the domestic and the global economy.

The mercantilist position is close to the realist view of international relations in stressing the subordination of economic forces to political interests and in emphasising the reality and primacy of national interest. The general condition of the mercantilist school is that of international anarchy tempered by war and diplomacy. Contemporary Europe sees economic policy as a weapon in the struggle for security and dominance between states. Therefore, we only have an apparent international state system constraining international economics. In reality we have politics constraining economics, since mercantilism and realism absolutely deny an international interest.

This particular both politic and economic attitude also has implications for domestic economic activity as the opposition to the unrestricted expansion by multinational corporations into the domestic market as abroad. Mercantilist states in contemporary Europe such as Britain, France, Germany and the Low Countries, work hard, through either economic or politic dispositions, to prevent foreign interests from acquiring the ability to manipulate the domestic economy or to deny supplies of strategically important materials and even to prevent them from reducing the nation-state effectiveness and the possibility of forced dealings in international affairs. Therefore, it seems that the mercantilist "power perspective" is opposed at all important points and values of liberal trade theory and practice. Economic realism, and its neo-mercantilist corollary, thus offers a significantly changing view of economic reality. Its claims to acceptance rest more upon is essential realism rather than theoretical formulations. It offers not so much a rigorous theory but, rather, a realistic disposition which can permit a less doctrinaire view of a wide range of policies and practices that are often adopted in the real world.

Now many cases of practical mercantilism can be enumerated which particularly interest European states. Most of European countries draw a large sum of their profits through well organised multinational companies in their colonial territories. Since the last two decades multinational co-operation was directed to buy past markets in those less developed countries and get cheaper labour wanting to create a new and better controlled market. One of the most remarkable example of this economic system is the British multinational RTZ, operating in Australia since the mid 1970s. RTZ has produced a remarkable devaluation of local economy by literally destroying environmental resources local people lived on. Pollution caused by opening new mines seriously damaged local fishery, agriculture and breeding reducing local population to famine. Even though the government involvement is denied it is noticeably there, since 16th% of RTZ profits goes to the government. Here three invested interest can be found, British government, Australian government and RTZ. British government wants to protect RTZ interests in an explicit way by renewing advantageous economic links with Australian economy and never taking care of the environmental degradation. Multinational cooperation finds its justification in the principle that the right on a land depends on the ability to defend it.

The Anglo-Dutch oil multinational Shell is another example of practical mercantilism in contemporary Europe. Shell is the leading player in trade between Britain and Nigeria. It extracts about half of the country`s oil production and 14% of Shell`s world-wide production of crude oil comes from Nigeria. In November 1995 Shell has set to sign a £4 billion deal with Nigeria for a huge new natural gas plant, despite world outrage and the threat of trade sanctions over the execution of the Ogoni playwright Ken Saro-Wiwa and Nigeria`s suspension from the Commonwealth. Saro Wiwa was executed with eight other opposition figures by the government of the dictator General Sani Abacha after being accused of complicity in the murder of four Nigerian government officials in Ogoniland, one of Nigeria`s main oil-producing areas. He was a key figure in Ogoni demands for compensation for the pollution of land by the oil industry and a higher share for Ogoni people of government oil revenues. Farmers' activity in Ogony is no more possible since both water and soil have been polluted and while soil products are now difficult to grow, cattle dies by famine and polluted water. Many pressures have been made demanding international sanctions, a complete arms embargo against Nigeria, a gradual turn-off of oil exports, and a freeze on Nigerian`s Ministers' bank accounts abroad. Despite EU sanctions adopted in 1993 Britain continues to send arms to Nigeria. British government denies any possible involvement with Abacha's military regime. However Nigeria is Britain`s 36th largest world market, taking £485m in exports from the UK in 1994, with imports of £125m. The invested interests in this trade are the governments of Britain, Netherland and Nigeria, the Commonwealth and Shell itself. However, Europe can be seen as another invested interest since many sanction acts and punitive measures are often evaded.

There are important economic reasons for Europe supporting Shell. Many modern fertilisers derive from oil refinement. A sudden lack of oil would mean many troubles for agriculture in all the industrialised West.

The achievement of control, whether unilaterally or through co-operation with other actors, may bring considerable advantages. Indeed, effective control is, however, a far from unproblematic matter. The resources necessary for unilateral control may be unattainable. It is the conflict that may arise between many of the actors on the global scene, and the fatal defections that undermine many of their cooperative efforts, that create the need for communities to look towards their own resources and to avoid becoming over-reliant upon external sources of wellbeing and succour.

The Economic Realists recognise that international collaboration to control and regulate the economic environment is highly desirable. However, enthusiasm for any form of international collaboration, whether through formal agreement or the tacit acceptance of international trade, should always be tempered and prior regard paid to the protection of one's own society's interests and wellbeing. The development of many of the institutions and rules of the EEC can be viewed as the cautious attempt to construct a tighter and more reassuring form of cooperative international association through Europe.

In the political realm, the maintenance of military forces has long been recognised as the norm for those states that have a serious regard for their economic security and sovereignty. This and other means are used by those powerful nation-states which intend to continue and reinforce their trade. A variety of protectionist measures, including tariffs, quotas and non-tariff barriers, have been used with considerable success to cushion infant industries or to provide an umbrella under which competitiveness can be restored in the face of growing international competition. Countries may be persuaded to moderate their export to another country by the possibility that trade barriers will be imposed. Agreements can also be reached on restraints that remain within acceptable, if not ideal, limits. A wide variety of measures may also be adopted to support and promote a country exports such as insurance schemes, credits and direct subsidies.

Reality continues to confront even those governments that would favour the total abolition of all neo-mercantilist policies and practices. A wide range of domestic conditions, and thereby governmental policy, continue to have a profound influence upon the international competitiveness and economic wellbeing of societies. Behaviour that is effectively mercantilist is, therefore, extremely widespread in the modern Europe and governments cannot ignore the benefits that others secure when such behaviour is effectively orchestrated. By the other side, the governments of many Less Developed Countries remain seriously constrained by weaknesses, financial, industrial and organisational. Most of the times the only chance these countries are given is to choose whether to exploit those opportunities with which they are presented.

There is a behaviour that states may undertake which, despite having little apparent connection with mercantilism, may have profound significance for the promotion of this political and economic system. Such behaviour ranges from the provision of "aid", through the relative subtlety of educational and cultural contacts, to the somewhat cruder promotion of arms sales. This happened in the case of France towards North and North-West African countries and all its past colonies as the French Guiana in South America. The same happened for Belgium towards Central-African states, for the Netherland in South America and the Middle East, and finally for Britain towards the Commonwealth and every inch of its past Colonial Empire.

In all these cases aid has been identified with the maintenance of control and influence over "recipient countries". Many forms of aid have sometimes been thought to be free from manipulative possibilities. However, many critics of the World Bank and the World Bank's affiliates have identified a strongly conservative bias in their policies which has seriously damaged the interests and developmental prospects of many of those LDCs that have been involved with these organisations.

Educational and cultural contacts allow societies to exert a low-key influence over the populations and the leading members of the countries. Such sources of influence can be seen as a form of cultural imperialism which is irresistible, save to those countries that consciously resist to such a contamination, as Iran.

Finally, the promotion of foreign arms sales in LDCs is an activity in which European governments participate energetically. Moreover, private arms sales go on with a degree of tacit governmental toleration.

Media play an important role in defending and promoting mercantilism in the Western Hemisphere and in creating a new information imperialism. Facts from the third world are often distorted and presented under a false neutrality. This is the case in which established forces are threatened by the true. Because of deforestation, many people died in flooding and mud slides in areas with no previous experiences of natural calamity. At the same time coral reefs are poisoned with cyanide to provide goldfish for the goldfish market in Europe and the United States. Africa`s recurring famines and poverty have political roots in the west. During 1985 we were informed about the Ethiopian famine but many of us still do not know that that country, the hungriest in

Africa, gave twice as much money to us in the west, in interest payments, as we gave to them. Under the same principle of information imperialism, independence movements in the Less Developed Countries are always presented in a negative light in the western media, in the same way as terrorism is almost never associated with the west, only with the third world. Most of the British press is owned by oligarchies in the making: the Maxwells, Murdoch, Blakenham. Serious measures were taken towards occasional programmes digressing from the orthodoxy of legitimacy.

Mercantilism can thus be seen as the post-cold war recolonization. Shiraz Kissam wrote that "The global news giants prescribe us information …. like the explorers who preceded them, they are mapping the world on a principle of perpetual extension. Hence, the globe is seen in terms of the west's need for it.".

The most objective conclusion can only be that in contemporary Europe the ideal of free market is basically linked to the power of capital and for this reason market could not be free.

Bibliography

- Amin, Ash and John Tomaney eds., *Behind the Myth of European Union*, Routledge, 1995.

- Barry Jones, R.J., *Conflict and Control in the World Economy, Contemporary Economic Realism & Neo-Mercantilism*, Humanities Press International Inc., Atlantic Highlands, N.J.1986.

- Pilger, J., *Information is Power*, New Statesman and Society: 15 November 1991 :10-11, London.

- Serberny-Mohammed A., *The Global and the Local International Communications*, Mass Media and Society: 118-150, Curran & Gurevitch eds.,1992.

- Waites, Bernard ed., *Europe and the Wider World*, ed. Strange the Printer Ltd., London 1980.

- *Economic Growth and Planning*, p. 904-33; *Economic Systems*, p.934-38. Britannica

Macropaedia, vol. 17, Encyclopaedia Britannica Inc., Chicago 1990.

~ *Neo-Mercantilism*, p.704-5, Collier`s Encyclopaedia, vol. 15, Macmillan Educational Company, New York 1984.

www.ingramcontent.com/pod-product-compliance
Lightning Source LLC
Chambersburg PA
CBHW031524210526
45464CB00007B/3021